SEE IT GROW!

See a Mushroom Grow

by Kirsten Chang

BELLWETHER MEDIA · MINNEAPOLIS, MN

Blastoff! Readers are carefully developed by literacy experts to build reading stamina and move students toward fluency by combining standards-based content with developmentally appropriate text.

 Level 1 provides the most support through repetition of high-frequency words, light text, predictable sentence patterns, and strong visual support.

 Level 2 offers early readers a bit more challenge through varied sentences, increased text load, and text-supportive special features.

 Level 3 advances early-fluent readers toward fluency through increased text load, less reliance on photos, advancing concepts, longer sentences, and more complex special features.

★ **Blastoff! Universe**

Reading Level

Grade **K**

Grades **1–3**

Grade **4**

This edition first published in 2023 by Bellwether Media, Inc.

No part of this publication may be reproduced in whole or in part without written permission of the publisher. For information regarding permission, write to Bellwether Media, Inc., Attention: Permissions Department, 6012 Blue Circle Drive, Minnetonka, MN 55343.

Library of Congress Cataloging-in-Publication Data

LC record for See a Mushroom Grow available at http://lccn.loc.gov/2022039511

Editor: Betsy Rathburn   Designer: Brittany McIntosh

Printed in the United States of America, North Mankato, MN.

Table of Contents

Cool and Damp

It is cool
and **damp**.
Mushrooms
are growing!

How Do They Grow?

Mushrooms are **fungi**. They often grow in dead plant matter.

Needed to Grow

coolness

dampness

dead
plant matter

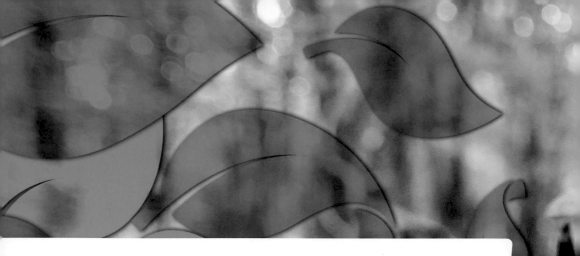

Mushrooms grow fast. Some can double their size in one day!

They start
as tiny **spores**.
The spores grow
long, white strings.

spore

The white strings
form **stalks**.
The stalks grow.

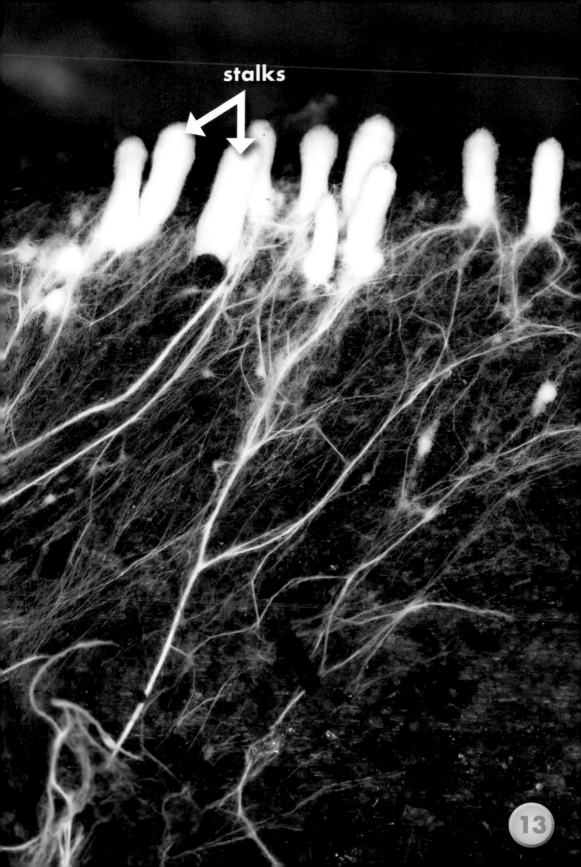

stalks

Caps form on top of the stalks. Most caps have **gills**.

cap

gills

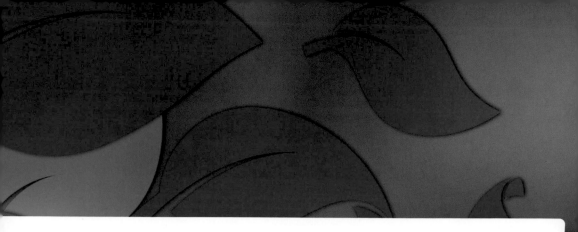

The mushrooms
let out spores
from their caps or gills.
More mushrooms
will grow!

spores

Fully Grown

Some mushrooms taste good. Some are used to make ink!

Using Mushrooms

tea

pizza
topping

ink

Mushrooms are
interesting fungi.
They come in
many shapes
and sizes!

Mushroom Life Cycle

1 spores grow long, white strings

2 strings form stalks

3 caps grow on the stalks

4 mushrooms let out spores

21

Glossary

caps

the tops of mushrooms

gills

parts of a mushroom below the cap that let out spores

damp

slightly wet

spores

tiny things that grow into fungi

fungi

living things that grow from spores

stalks

long, skinny parts of mushrooms

To Learn More

AT THE LIBRARY

Markovics, Joyce L. *Mushrooms*. Chicago, Ill.: Norwood House Press, 2023.

Mikoley, Kate. *What Are Fungi?* New York, N.Y.: Gareth Stevens Publishing, 2020.

Owings, Lisa. *From Spore to Mushroom*. Minneapolis, Minn.: Lerner Publications, 2018.

ON THE WEB

FACTSURFER

Factsurfer.com gives you a safe, fun way to find more information.

1. Go to www.factsurfer.com.

2. Enter "see a mushroom grow" into the search box and click 🔍.

3. Select your book cover to see a list of related content.

Index

The images in this book are reproduced through the courtesy of: MarLein, front cover (spores); zhu difeng, front cover (small mushroom); Kyselova Inna, front cover (mushroom); stocksolutions, p. 3; Shaiith, pp. 4-5; Ledanip, pp. 6-7; Jesse Stephens, p. 7 (top left); TTstudio, p. 7 (top middle); Bewickswan, p. 7 (top right); Sertan Yaman, pp. 8-9; Dmytro_Ostapenko, pp. 10-11; Mindhive, p. 11 (top); Kichigin, pp. 12-13, 22 (spores); Maksim Safaniuk, pp. 14-15; Melesandre, p. 15 (bottom); godi photo, pp. 16-17; Prostock-studio, pp. 18-19; seagames50 images, p. 19 (top left); GSDesign, p. 19 (top middle); bogdan ionescu, p. 19 (top right); GIOIA PHOTO, pp. 20-21; Nikolay Zaborskikh, p. 22 (caps); Erazem Dolzan, p. 22 (damp); Kisova Elena, p. 22 (fungi); ressormat, p. 22 (gills); Upadim, p. 22 (stalks); ANCH, p. 23.